Edward M. Allen

La Fayette's Second Expedition to Virginia in 1781

A paper read before the Maryland historical society, June 14th, 1886

Edward M. Allen

La Fayette's Second Expedition to Virginia in 1781
A paper read before the Maryland historical society, June 14th, 1886

ISBN/EAN: 9783337324032

Printed in Europe, USA, Canada, Australia, Japan

Cover: Foto ©Andreas Hilbeck / pixelio.de

More available books at **www.hansebooks.com**

Fund-Publication, No. 32.

LA FAYETTE'S
SECOND EXPEDITION TO VIRGINIA
IN 1781.

A Paper read before the Maryland Historical Society,

June 14th, 1886,

By E. M. ALLEN.

Baltimore, 1891.

PEABODY PUBLICATION FUND.

COMMITTEE ON PUBLICATION.

1891–92.

HENRY STOCKBRIDGE,

BRADLEY T. JOHNSON,

CLAYTON C. HALL.

PRINTED BY JOHN MURPHY & CO.
PRINTERS TO THE MARYLAND HISTORICAL SOCIETY.
BALTIMORE, 1891.

LA FAYETTE'S SECOND EXPEDITION
TO VIRGINIA IN 1781.

IT has been said that there was, properly, no *second* expedition to Virginia led by La Fayette, because the troops under his command that proceeded from Elkton by water on the way to Virginia, only went as far as Annapolis; but as La Fayette himself went to Virginia at that time, and, as the whole body returned to Elkton and started again under fresh orders from the commander-in-chief, and with a different object, I deem it proper to call the expedition that went by land, and which reached Virginia, the *Second Expedition.*

As far as I know, no connected account of this expedition has been written, including the part taken by La Fayette individually, and by the troops he commanded, and I regard it as consonant with the objects of this organization to preserve in a form easily accessible, all facts that will enable those who are to succeed us to have full

5

knowledge of even the minute circumstances connected with the Revolutionary struggle.

In order, therefore, to enable the student to comprehend the importance of the expedition which is the subject of this paper, it is necessary to place before him the situation of the country, and the prospects of the American cause in the beginning of the year 1781, including the state of public sentiment, the condition of the finances, the situation and strength of the armies, and the objects of the campaign of that year.

We had fought many battles since blood was first shed at Lexington in 1775. Bunker Hill, Trenton, Brandywine, Camden, and King's Mountain, and other bloody fields had attested the determination of the American people to be a free and independent nation ; yet no battle like Zama or the Boyne, or Waterloo, had changed the policy and the hopes of the nations that contended for supremacy on the American continent.

The war had been waged more than five years ; yet nothing had appeared to lift the gloom that shrouded the American cause, save the French alliance and the French material aid. There was not even a confederation of the states, for Maryland, the last State to give in her adhesion to that flimsy compact, had not yet done so.

The want of a concentrated federal power threatened total ruin to the cause of Independence, and it may be safely said, that to ordinary human calculation, it was unwise to continue the contest.

The treasury was empty. The British had flooded the country with counterfeits of the American currency, and ten millions of dollars issued by Congress had to be called in from this cause.

I have seen a bill in which four hundred dollars was charged for a pair of boots, and one hundred dollars for a handkerchief, about that time, in the paper issues of the Government.

Calls made upon the states for men and money were often disregarded, and in general the response was dilatory and feeble.

Congress in 1779 called for eighty battalions to recruit the army. Not one of the states filled its quota, but Massachusetts led the states in responding to this call.

Many of the people, in all the states, openly aided the cause of the mother country, and more secretly wished it success in its efforts to crush out the infant Government.

The troops of Connecticut had mutinied, and the Pennsylvania line, their spirits depressed by thoughts of their needy families, with no pay, upon the verge of starvation in camp, and a vigilant and well provided enemy in front, had followed the pernicious example.

The general gloom had been increased by the treason of Arnold, and even the execution of André had been made by some of the wavering a justification for returning to their allegiance to the British crown, and it may well be said that "shadows, clouds and darkness" rested upon the land.

But the clouds had a silver lining.

That sturdy love of liberty that led the pilgrims from home and friends, and the graves of their fathers, to brave the perils of an untrodden wilderness, and to scorn the tomahawk of the savage; that spirit that glowed in the breast of Hampden, and that nerved the arm of the immortal Cromwell, was still alive, and on that spirit rested the hopes of all the friends of liberty that this land would yet be the "land of the free," because it was the "home of the brave."

Lord George Germain, the British Secretary of State for the colonies, in a letter to Sir Henry Clinton, dated March 7th, 1781, says: "Indeed, so very contemptible is the rebel force in all its parts, and so vast is our superiority everywhere, that no resistance on their part is to be apprehended that can materially obstruct the progress of the King's armies in the speedy suppression of the rebellion; and it is a pleasing, though at the same time, mortifying reflection when the duration of the rebellion is considered, which arises from a view of the returns of the provincial forces you have transmitted, that the American levies in the King's service are more in number than the whole of the enlisted troops in the service of the congress."

But, "Man proposes and God disposes." God, who wills not that "Man's inhumanity to man" shall make "countless thousands mourn" to the end of time, but wills that all men shall have life, liberty and the pursuit of happiness in their own way, had given us to guide us in council and to lead us on the field of battle, that man, whose name is destined to be hallowed among all the generations of mankind—George Washington!

On him the people leaned. His unshaken faith in ultimate triumph, his perfect rectitude, his dignity and his blameless life, commanded the confidence and justified the hopes of our patriotic fathers. The army had almost ceased to exist, and only two armed vessels remained of the navy; the others had been captured or destroyed.

While the affairs of the states were in this desperate condition, General Clinton, who commanded the British forces in America, determined to send an expedition to Virginia under the traitor Arnold, consisting of a fleet of armed vessels and land forces to coöperate with it, in order to subjugate what was then the most important member of the Confederacy.

General Washington sent General La Fayette with a detachment from the main army in New

Jersey, to capture Arnold, if possible, and at least to impede his progress and circumscribe the area of his operations.

La Fayette had passed from Elkton to Annapolis in boats with his troops, and after a reconnoisance in Virginia, he was compelled to return to Elkton, because the French fleet that had been sent from Newport, R. I., under the Chevalier Destouches to coöperate with him, had been unsuccessful in an engagement with the British fleet under Admiral Arbuthnot off the capes of the Chesapeake, and had returned to Newport, leaving Arbuthnot with a superior naval force, in the Chesapeake Bay.

On the return of La Fayette to Elkton, the return also having been made by water, he received the following letter of instructions from the commander-in-chief:

"NEW WINDSOR, 6 *Apr.*, 1781.

" *My Dear Marquis,*—

"Since my letter to you of yesterday I have attentively considered of what vast importance it will be to reinforce General Greene as speedily as possible; more especially as there can be but little doubt that the detachment under General Philips, if not part of that under the command of General Arnold, will ultimately join or in some degree coöperate with Lord Cornwallis. [Philips and Arnold were at this time in Virginia, and Cornwallis was in the Carolinas.] I have communicated to the general officers at present with the army, my sentiments on the subject; and they are unanimously of opinion that the detachment under your command should proceed to join the Southern Army. Your being already three hundred miles advanced, which is nearly half way, is the reason that operates against any that can be offered in favor of marching that detachment back, you will therefore immediately on the receipt of this, turn the detachment to the southward.

"Inform General Greene that you are upon your march to join him, and take his direction as to your route, when you begin to approach him.

"Previously to that, you will be guided by your own judgment, and by the roads on which you will be most likely to find subsistence for the troops and horses.

"It will be well to advise Governor Jefferson of your intended march through the State of Virginia; or perhaps it might answer a good purpose were you to go forward to Richmond yourself, after putting the troops in motion and having made some necessary arrangements for their progress. You will take with you the light artillery and smallest mortars with their stores and the musket cartridges.

"But let these follow under a proper escort, rather than impede the march of the detachment, which ought to move as expeditiously as possible without injury to them.

"The heavy artillery and stores you will leave at some proper and safe place, if it cannot be conveniently transported to Christiana River, from whence it can easily be got to Philadelphia. You may leave it to the option of Lieut.-Colonel Stevens to proceed or not as he may think proper. His family is in peculiar circumstances, and he left in the expectation of being absent but a short time.

"Should there be other officers under similar circumstances, you may make them the same offers, and they shall be relieved.

"I will now mention to you in confidence, the true reason which operated with me, more than almost any other, in favor of recalling your detachment and forming another.

"It was the uneasiness among the field officers of those regiments which furnished the men, upon the appointment of Colonel Gimat and Major Galvan to commands in the corps.

"They presented a memorial to me upon the subject, and I gave them the true reason, which was, that the regiments in their lines were so extremely thin of field officers of their own, that necessity, if nothing else, dictated the measure.

" I have heard nothing of the discontent lately; but should I find it revive again upon its being known that the corps is to continue together, I shall be obliged, for peace sake, to relieve those two gentlemen by officers properly belonging to the lines from which the regiments were formed. You will therefore prepare them for such an event, and tell them candidly the reasons, founded principally upon their having already had their tour in the infantry.

" Should they be relieved, they will probably incline to continue with the Southern Army.

" There is as much or more probability of their finding employment there, than with us, as we shall, from all appearances, remain inactive.

" I am, my dear Marquis, &c.,

" GEO. WASHINGTON."

It will be observed that this letter of instructions is dated April 6th, at New Windsor, in Connecticut, distant about one hundred and fifteen miles east from New York, and therefore about two hundred and fifty miles from Elkton, where La Fayette received it. It is fair to presume that in those days of slow conveyance, several days were required to traverse this distance with horses,

2

which furnished the swiftest conveyance in the days of the American Revolution.

The letter from Washington giving the order for the return southward being dated April 6th, two hundred and fifty miles away, the fact that La Fayette was on the march on April 11th is a striking proof of the promptness of La Fayette in giving effect to even disagreeable orders, for he preferred to operate at this time in the North.

He left Elkton on the 11th of April, having under his command the following troops, as near as now can be ascertained:

INFANTRY.

Major-General Marquis De La Fayette.
Division Inspector, Major Wm. Barber, of New Jersey.

FIRST BRIGADE.

Brigade Major, Captain John Hobby, Tenth Massachusetts.

First Battalion.

Colonel Joseph Vose, of Massachusetts.
Major Caleb Gibbs, of Rhode Island.
Eight Massachusetts companies.

Second Battalion.

Lieutenant-Colonel Gimat.
Major John Palsgrave Wyllys, of Connecticut.

Five companies. Four Massachusetts and one Rhode Island company.

Third Battalion.

Lieutenant-Colonel Francis Barber, of New Jersey.
Major Jos. R. Reed (of H———), New Jersey.
Five companies. New Hampshire and New Jersey troops.

SECOND BRIGADE.

Brevet Brigadier-General Moses Hazen, of Canada.
Brigade Major, Captain Leonard Bleeker, First New York.

First Battalion.

Lieutenant-Colonel Ebenezer Huntingdon, of Connecticut.
Major Nathan Rice, of Massachusetts.
Four companies. Massachusetts and Connecticut troops.

Second Battalion.

Lieutenant-Colonel Alexander Hamilton, of New York.
Major Nicholas Fish, of New York.
Four companies. Two New York and two Connecticut troops.

Third Battalion.

Lieutenant-Colonel John Laurens, of South Carolina.
Major John N. Cumming, of New Jersey.
Four companies. New Hampshire, Massachusetts, and Connecticut.

Fourth Battalion.

Lieutenant-Colonel Edward Antrill.
Major Tarleton Woodson.
Hazen's Canadian Regiment.

The names of all the aids of the division commanders do not appear. In the campaign, La Fayette had Majors George Washington (nephew of General Washington), Richard C. Anderson and Wm. Archibald, of Virginia, and Captain Angus Grème, an officer of the French Army.

La Fayette, in his memoirs, says the richest young men of Virginia and Maryland had come to join him as volunteer dragoons: and from their intelligence, as well as from the superiority of their horses, they were of essential service to him.

But while the army records show that La Fayette's division comprised these at the siege of Yorktown, it is known that at least one of the officers named here was not with the army on its march through Maryland. This officer was Alexander Hamilton, a man whose talents and virtues entitled him to the proud position among the sons of men, given him by that supreme judge of human capabilities—the renowned Talleyrand.

Talleyrand, when in this country in 1794, seeing Hamilton at work in his office late at night, said: "I have seen one of the wonders of the world, I have seen a man laboring all night to support his family, who has made the fortune of a nation. I consider Napoleon, Fox and Hamilton the three greatest men of our epoch, and without hesitation I award the first place to Hamilton."

Hamilton became, on the death of Washington, commander-in-chief of the armies of the United States.

La Fayette wrote a letter in the old house still standing near Bald Friar, in Harford county, to Hamilton, in which he expressed the hope that he would remain with Washington, but entreating him, in case he took service in the field, to join *him* in the South. It is certain, therefore, that Hamilton was not then with him in Harford county, but that he joined him afterwards is equally certain. La Fayette himself, after leaving Elkton, passed the first night at the house of Job Haines, near Rising Sun, while part of his troops encamped at the Brick Meeting-house, and another part near Rising Sun in Cecil county.

It is among the traditions of the neighborhood, that on leaving Mr. Haines', after spending the night there, he gave each of Haines' sons a piece of money.

To one of the sons, named Louis, he gave a gold piece, because he was of the same name as La Fayette's sovereign, the unfortunate Louis XVI.

The next day they crossed the Susquehanna at Bald Friar, where La Fayette became the guest of Colonel James Rigby, then one of the chief citizens of Harford county.

Colonel Rigby seems to have been a man of importance in his day, for there is still standing near his house a log building that was used as a jail in his time.

It seems to be constructed of yellow poplar logs, laid close together, and it was, doubtless, when in good order, a secure place of confinement for ordinary criminals who were without edge tools.

Colonel Rigby seems to have had no sons who had descendants. The name has therefore disappeared from the county, as far as I know; but his descendants remain with other names, one of his great grandsons being James Rigby Massey, Esq., a highly respected citizen of the region in which his distinguished ancestor dwelt. I trust I shall be excused for giving even the minutest details of this expedition, for I believe that what is interesting to myself in connection with the great events of our history, will be interesting to most men in the years that are to come.

As I stated in a former page, the affairs of our struggling country were in an almost hopeless condition.

The troops with La Fayette were from the northern states—some of them even from Canada, and they had shown great aversion to a southern campaign. They were on the verge of mutiny, and it was predicted with confidence, that not half of his force would be with him when he reached Baltimore.

The heart of La Fayette was full of a lofty confidence; but we who enjoy the fruition of his labors can imagine the difficulties of his position and thank God that he was gifted with such signal power to meet them.

In imagination we can go back to that night in the early spring of 1781, and to the capacious fireplace with its blazing logs in the old Rigby mansion.

The old fireplace was in one of those wonderful chimneys that seem to have been the pride of our forefathers, and has been a marvel to persons now living. The present owner of the property pulled it down some years ago, and after building from it a modern chimney, had bricks enough from it to build a capacious outbuilding, and great store of bricks left over.

In the fields about the house the men and horses had such food and shelter as their scanty commissariat afforded. A consultation was held. General Hazen was there, and Colonels Vose and Gimat, Barber, Huntingdon and the other field officers.

What was to be done to stop desertion? A proclamation was prepared that night in this old house that may have achieved the independence of the United States of America!

Who can tell the influence of the act most insignificant in the lives of men, or in the history of nations?

Jefferson used to say that we were indebted to *flies* for the Declaration of Independence.

He said that after much debate in Congress, it was found impossible to come to a vote on the declaration by reason of the parliamentary tactics of the opposition. Delay was increasing the strength of the friends of the old government, when on a hot summer afternoon a great gust of wind and rain approached. The heat was great, and the stocking-covered legs of the grave congressmen were besieged by hungry flies.

They beat their limbs with their bandannas, in vain efforts to obtain relief. The friends of independence saw their opportunity and proposed an immediate vote.

Rather than endure such torment, a vote was allowed, and independence was carried. Jefferson expressed the belief that if there had been no flies, there would have been no independence.

What would have been the fate of France if Grouchy had not mistaken Bonaparte's orders at Waterloo?

Had Richard Cromwell possessed the ability of his great sire, what would have been the history of England for the last two hundred years?

If Williams, Van Wart and Paulding had been corrupt, what would have been our own history since the treason of Arnold?

If La Fayette and his officers had not devised a plan by which desertion was ended in the army under his orders, it is probable that Cornwallis would not have been captured, and as a consequence the American colonies might have been still dependencies of Great Britain.

They determined to appeal to the noblest feelings of the soldiers, not to their fears, not to their greed of gain.

La Fayette, from this old house in Harford county, issued a proclamation in which he stated that he was on his way to meet and fight a powerful foe. That for himself, no diminution of numbers would deter him, but that in firm reliance upon the God of battles, and the justice of the American cause, he would continue his march to meet the enemy.

He closed by offering a free pass to every soldier who would apply for it at headquarters, by which he might go home.

Not one man availed of this offer, and from that time desertions ceased. But La Fayette's conduct on this occasion reminds us of the exhortation of Cromwell to his soldiers—"Trust in God, but keep your powder dry," for he hung one soldier and disgraced another who had been caught, after a previous desertion.

His trust was not *altogether* in the smiles of Providence, or in the honor of his troops.

In the passage of the river, the scow which La Fayette was in ran aground before dry land was reached, and Aquilla Deaver, a man known to men whom I have known, carried him from the scow to the shore on his back.

Deaver went to Port Deposit in 1824 to see La Fayette, when he held a reception there.

He told the General that he was the man who had carried him to the Harford shore on his back, La Fayette remembered him and greeted him with great cordiality.

This old soldier lived, in the latter part of his life, in a house afterwards for many years owned and occupied by Samuel Harwood, and now owned by Jeremiah P. Silver. Esq., in the second district of Harford county.

One of his grandsons, now living, lately gave me some account of the old gentleman.

He seems to have been a philosopher, as well as a patriot, for his grandson states that in his latter years he received a pension as a revolutionary soldier, and that, dwelling in peace, the only break in the monotony of his life was when, twice a year, his pension fell due. Then he would get up his horse and wagon and drive to Baltimore. There he would collect his pension and lay in a stock of the comforts of life sufficient to last until his pension would fall due again, and chief among these comforts was always an ample supply of whiskey.

By his own direction he was buried in a corner of his own land, where he lies in an unmarked grave, and I commend the marking of it with a stone, properly inscribed, to this organization, as a matter consonant with its objects.

An old man who paid his respects to La Fayette on this occasion, told me some circumstances connected with that reception, one of which was this: the general was exceedingly urbane in his deportment, and had something pleasant to say to each person who was presented to him.

The old man, who was not then old, said that when La Fayette took the hand of the man who was presented before *him*, he expressed his pleasure at seeing him, and said, "Are you a married man?" Receiving an affirmative reply, he said, "Happy man." And when my informant immediately followed, La Fayette asked him the same question. He replied that he was not married, when La Fayette said "*Lucky dog*," and, smiling, greeted the next in the line of his grateful admirers.

It is not common for commanders to march with the body of an army, unless when in the presence of the enemy, and La Fayette seems to have passed rapidly through Harford and Baltimore counties, to Baltimore, for we are told that he reached there at night after leaving Bald Friar, or Susquehanna Ferry, as he calls it, in the morning of the same day. He dined, however, at *Bush*, in Harford county, which information I have from an aged resident of that region whose father dwelt near Bush.

By way of showing the length of the links that connect us with the past, I will here state that I knew a lady well, in my early years, who met and talked with La Fayette on that day. She was with her brother on the way from Baltimore, and meeting La Fayette and his staff, they made some inquiries about the route. This old lady died in 1843, aged over eighty years, and she was therefore about twenty years old in 1781.

The troops marched by way of the Trappe Church, Priestford, and Bush, to Baltimore.

Before they reached the "Trappe" a trunk, said to contain coin, was lost from a baggage wagon. It was found by Reuben Jones, grandfather of some present residents of the fifth district of Harford county. Jones mounted a horse and, overtaking them, told them where the trunk was. They sent after it and Jones reproached them in language not polite, to the end of his days, for giving him no reward for the trouble he took.

There lived, a few years ago in Harford county, a gentleman whose father was on the staff of La Fayette in this march.

La Fayette did not command Frenchmen in the war of the Revolution, as some believe, but when he was ordered to Virginia with his detachment, he asked and obtained leave to take with him Colonel Gimat and Captain Grème, French officers then with the French troops in the United States.

A son of Captain Grème, who lived to a great age, and died in my house in 1880, has often related to me incidents connected with this march, told him by his father or family.

When the officers reached that part of the road that descends to Priestford, from the "Trappe" Church, they were enchanted with the beauty of the scene.

Far the greater part of the region they had traversed was rough and forbidding. The agriculture was rude and the roads were bad. Looking westward, in descending to Deer Creek, they beheld the beautiful valley that stretches across the creek and up Jericho and Thomas' runs. The morning was one of those that still bid man " Look through nature up to nature's God," in the early spring.

> " The flowers sprang, wanton to be pres't,
> The birds sang love on every spray."

The plodding husbandman, " drove his team afield," the herds grazed in peace in the grassy fields, and the lark, soaring high in air, chanted his morning song.

Colonel Gimat and Captain Grème had long been soldiers together, and the sufferings and triumphs of their profession had united them in more than a common friendship.

Gimat was a man of wealth, and death having robbed him in early life of her whose "witching smile" had caught his "youthful fancy," his chief aim was to seek some quiet spot, when wars alarms were past, where, in the company of his friend, he could be at peace.

The two friends then and there agreed that when the war was over, they would return to France, and, after arranging their affairs, they would return to America, buy the property, now the beautiful home of Dr. Magraw, and there,

"In the cool sequestered vale of life,"
Keep "the noiseless tenor of their way."

They did go home to France, and they did return, and purchased the property which they had selected as the home of their old age.

Gimat paid for it, and presented it to his friend, Grème, and they went back to France to make their final arrangements before leaving their old home forever.

They looked forward to many years in which each might "Shoulder his crutch and show how fields were won."

But "this world has no fulfilment for hopes that rise above it," and all their plans were frustrated.

That mighty *cyclone*, I may call it, the French Revolution of 1789 came on.

Napoleon Bonaparte, the mightiest of the race of man since Julius Cæsar, appeared upon the scene.

That wonderful man intoxicated the French people with the grandeur of his aspirations, and the marvels of his career.

Colonel Gimat and his friend, dazzled by the glory of France, and by the mighty achievements of her wonderful leader, deferred their return to America until peace and order should triumph over the horrors of the Revolution.

When order was restored at home, Gimat and Grème were induced to go with the French army to San Domingo to suppress the insurrection there.

Grème, in the meantime, had married in Paris, and taking his bride to Martinique, both intended to come from there to Maryland, when the insurrection was suppressed. But Colonel Gimat, the friend of Washington, the chosen companion of La Fayette, lost his life in San Domingo, falling a victim to the fury of the savage population of the island.

Grème did come, bringing with him his wife and several children, and he lived and died on the place he and his friend had chosen as the most beautiful spot they had seen in America. He lies buried, having died in 1800, in the grave-yard of the Trappe Church, in Harford county, where a stone marks his grave, having an inscription stating his connection with the army under La Fayette.

Colonel Gimat seems to have been one of those rare men, " born to blush unseen," who live in the conscientious performance of every duty.

He led one division of the American army in the assault at Yorktown, and Alexander Hamilton led the other. They both captured the positions they attacked before the French troops succeeded in the part assigned to them, and crowned themselves with honor.

But, in the isle of San Domingo, where so many thousands of brave Frenchmen sleep.

> " Where the flower of the orange blows,
>   And the fireflies glance in the myrtle boughs,"

rests the brave, the trusted, the honored, and the unfortunate Colonel Gimat.

Let every American, let every Frenchman, let every lover of the beautiful and the true in human character, cast a flower upon the grave of Colonel Gimat!

La Fayette was lionized in Baltimore, the chief citizens emulating each other in paying him such attentions as were due to his distinguished character.

A ball was given in his honor at the Assembly Rooms, then at the corner of Holliday and Fayette streets.

During the progress of the dance a lady asked La Fayette why he was so sad. He replied, that he could not enjoy the gayeties of the occasion, because his poor soldiers needed so many of even the necessaries of life, clothes being their chief want.

The lady replied, "We will supply them." Next day the ball-room was turned into a clothing manufactory, patriotic husbands and fathers supplied the material, and fair women plied the shears and the needle.

Colonel McHenry wrote to General Greene, April 16th, 1781, from Baltimore. "While I admire *your* policy, I have more than once pitied the Marquis' situation. His troops passed here yesterday, discontented almost to general desertion: destitute of shirts and proper equipments, and in most respects unprovided for a march. You know the Marquis, he has been with us two days; but in this time he adopted an expedient to conciliate them to a degree, that no one else would have thought of. To-day he signs a contract, binding himself to certain merchants of this place, for above two thousand guineas, to be disposed of in shirts, over-alls, and hats for the detachment.

"Without these, the army could not proceed, and with these he has managed to reconcile them to the service.

" He is also bent upon trying the power of novelty on their minds by giving to the march the air of a frolic.

" His troops will ride in wagons and carts from Elkridge Landing to the limits of this State, and how much farther he will continue this mode of movement, depends upon Virginia."

As stated by Colonel McHenry, at Baltimore he borrowed from merchants about two thousand pounds sterling, for which he gave them his personal obligation, payable two years after date.

This *time* was asked, as he states in a letter to Washington, dated April 18th, at Baltimore, in order to enable him to dispose of his estate to procure the means of repayment. The march from Baltimore was resumed, and on the 19th the troops encamped near Elkridge Landing, in sight of the place, where now a hundred trains a day, carrying thousands of passengers, and thousands of tons of merchandise, rush forward to and from the busy centres of population and commerce, propelled by, what was then, a force almost unknown. In crossing there in scows, one sank, and by this mishap, nine men were drowned.

They reached Alexandria on the 21st of April. There La Fayette bought some shoes for his needy troops, and they pursued their journey through Fredericksburg and arrived at Richmond on the 29th, where the detachment was joined by Baron

Steuben, General Muhlenberg, and the Virginia militia, commanded by General Nelson.

La Fayette had started on this expedition to reinforce General Greene in the states farther south, but movements had taken place that brought General Cornwallis to Virginia, and that State now demanded the full force of the armies for her defence.

Greene had met Cornwallis at Guilford Court-house, and the bloody battle had been fought at that place.

Cornwallis had been so reduced by that battle, and the long and exhausting marches preceding and following it, that his force had dwindled from near two thousand five hundred veteran troops, to but little more than fourteen hundred. He was in the midst of a hostile population, destitute of regular supplies, and encumbered with many sick and wounded. He was forced to seek a defensible position, where his exhausted troops might recuperate.

He therefore retreated to Wilmington, N. C., where he arrived on the 7th of April, the day after Washington wrote the letter instructing La Fayette to proceed to the South and reinforce General Greene.

His intention was, as soon as the vigor of his force was recruited, and reinforcements from Ireland, which he expected, arrived, to return to the highlands to endeavor to aid the operations of Lord Rawdon in South Carolina. His plans were disconcerted by intelligence that Greene had rapidly marched toward Camden, S. C.

Cornwallis was greatly troubled, and his despairing expressions are almost comical.

" My situation here." he wrote to Sir Henry Clinton, "is very distressing; Greene has taken advantage of my being obliged to come to this place, and has marched to South Carolina;" and further on he says, "I much fear that Lord Rawdon's posts will be so distant from each other, and his troops so scattered, as to put him in the greatest danger of being beaten in detail, and that the worst of consequences may happen to most of the troops out of Charleston."

It was too late to follow Greene with reasonable hope of averting the danger; before he could reach the scene of action the blow would have fallen.

After remaining several days at Wilmington, he decided to take advantage of the defenceless state in which Greene's southern march left Southeastern Virginia, to march into that region and form a junction with the force under General Phillips.

By this move he hoped to draw Greene away from Lord Rawdon and by the reduction of Virginia to make a great stride towards the subjugation of the whole country.

General Phillips was at Portsmouth, having under him three thousand five hundred men of that hardy material that forms the regulars of the British Army.

He left Portsmouth on the 16th of April, and proceeding up James River, reached Manchester, opposite Richmond, on the morning of April 30th, to find that La Fayette had reached there on the evening before.

La Fayette had been reinforced by two thousand militia, and sixty dragoons, and he posted himself strongly on the high banks that commanded the south side of the river.

History affords few more striking illustrations of the uncertainty of man's judgment, than the results of this memorable campaign afford.

Here was La Fayette, a youth, twenty-three years of age, with little experience in the science of war, commanding an inferior force, *in numbers,* and inferior in a greater degree in all that makes it possible for commanders to organize victory in the cabinet.

His forces, in the sense in which the British were regulars, men trained in the manual of arms and to the hardships of the life of the soldier in the field by long service, were all of them merely raw militia-men. About two thousand were soldiers called regulars, because they had enlisted for longer terms than the transient levies that shouldered the musket when their homes were invaded, and, when the enemy left that immediate region, went home to tell the news. The remainder were of the kind last described. Opposed to him was Cornwallis, a veteran General of the regular British Army, of twice the age of La Fayette, yet still in the matured strength of vigorous life.

Cornwallis wrote to Sir Henry Clinton, at New York, " The boy cannot escape me," and " La Fayette cannot, I think, escape him," wrote Sir Henry Clinton to Lord George Germain, the British Colonial Secretary of State.

Here we see contempt for his adversary shown by this lordly soldier of the Crown, while La Fayette writes to his beloved chief that he had a " profound distrust of *himself*."

La Fayette, conscious of the superiority of the British Regulars in the open field, warily avoided an engagement, and marching northward formed a junction with General Wayne on the Rapidan.

Cornwallis, after the return of two ravaging expeditions which he had sent out under active officers, established his headquarters at Elk Hill, a plantation of Gov. Jefferson.

Thence he marched down the river to Williamsburg, where he arrived on the 25th of June.

An express from Sir Henry Clinton obliged Cornwallis to change his plans.

Washington threatened New York, and Clinton required Cornwallis to send him part of his troops for its protection.

It is a singular fact, that while Washington had no purpose to attack New York, his demonstrations against that place, which he made for the purpose of creating a diversion in favor of General Greene, by inducing Clinton to withdraw part of the British troops in the South to protect that city, had produced effects far more beneficial than he expected.

It is true, that at a conference held at Wethersfield on the 22d of May, between Washington and Rochambeau, it was decided that a concentration of the French and American forces in the neighborhood of New York was advisable, in order to be ready to take advantage of any opportunity which the weakness of the enemy might afford.

Yet it was not deemed wise to attack that place unless the force there was further weakened, and it was not further weakened, therefore there was no probability of such an attack. Clinton was alarmed. He wrote to Cornwallis, then at Williamsburg, Va., on the 11th of June, that New York was the object of attack by the combined French and American Armies, and required Cornwallis to send him three thousand troops from his command. Clinton wrote him that there was no prospect of reëstablishing the power of the Crown in Virginia, so general was the disaffection there, and advised him to take any healthy position he chose.

On the 4th of July he took up his march to Portsmouth, which position he chose, because, if reduced to extremities, it afforded a chance of a retreat to the Carolinas.

His engineers, after the most extensive surveys, reported that ships in Hampton Roads would not be secured by works on Point Comfort, and Clinton had told General Phillips on his embarkation for the Chesapeake in April, that there was no place so proper as Yorktown for the protection of the King's ships.

As the successor in the command in Virginia, General Phillips having died in May, he felt bound by Clinton's opinions, in the absence of specific orders. Cornwallis earnestly advised Clinton against the establishment of a defensive post on the Chesapeake, and asked leave to give up the command to General Leslie, and for himself to go back to Charleston.

These requests were denied him, and on the 12th of July, he was directed to hasten the embarkation of the three thousand men ordered to New York.

Early in August, Cornwallis embarked his troops, and leaving Portsmouth, passed up the bay and landed his whole force at Yorktown.

Clinton had intercepted letters, written to deceive him, in which the attack on New York was stated to be the main object of the campaign.

It must be borne in mind that the intention of Washington up to this time was merely to prevent succor being sent from New York to the British commanders in Virginia, and further south.

But the lives of men are in the main alike, whether the individual has in hand the forces and the destinies of nations, or controls only the simple and the feeble means and forces of the humble dweller in the lowly cottage.

The vast future is opened to man by slow degrees; often his way seems barred by objects that appear to stop all further progress; then suddenly all difficulties vanish, and at other times, when all his wisdom has been exercised to give direction to his powers, the scene shifts as suddenly as the aspect of the sunset glow, and all his plans and labors must be shaped anew.

A son of General Rochambeau arrived at this time in the United States with the intelligence that the Count De Grasse had left the harbor of Brest, in France, destined for the French possessions in the West Indies, and that he had orders to sail to the United States in July or August.

The French frigate, "Concorde," arrived at Newport shortly after, with despatches from De Grasse, stating that he would leave San Domingo on the 3d of August with twenty-five or thirty ships of the line, and a considerable land force, and that he would steer for the Chesapeake.

This changed the state of affairs, and the American and French commanders at once determined that all the French Army, and a large part of the American troops, should proceed at once to Virginia, and the Count De Barras, then at Newport, also determined to join De Grasse in the Chesapeake Bay.

Washington wrote to De Grasse, expecting his letter to find him in the Chesapeake, to send all the transports possible to Elkton (Head of Elk) by the 8th of September.

General Heath was put in command of West Point.

The utmost secresy was observed and camps were marked out, ovens for baking bread were erected, and every preparation was made in New Jersey, as if the army would occupy that State in force. Late in August they turned their faces southward.

Clinton's eyes were at last opened. He resolved to make a serious raid into Connecticut in the hope that at least part of Washington's force would be faced about to save that State.

The command of this expedition was given to Arnold, who executed the orders of his chief with his accustomed vigor and success, and in that raid he, who before was a traitor, earned additional ignominy by the massacre of the brave Ledyard and his soldiers at Fort Griswold.

Washington reached Philadelphia on the 30th of August, where he was received with every demonstration of confidence and affection, but the people wondered at the object of his visit. A ray of light had broken in the clouded sky of the nation; yet great difficulties existed still.

The troops gave evidences of discontent, their pay being long in arrears, and to march southward had always been distasteful to the troops from the North.

Even a small sum of money, it was thought, if judiciously employed amongst them, would put them in more cheerful mood.

The treasury of the nation was empty, and Morris, the financier, could supply no funds.

In this emergency, General Rochambeau came to the relief of Washington and loaned him twenty thousand dollars, which Morris engaged to pay by the 1st of October.

About this time Laurens arrived at Boston with about six hundred thousand dollars in coin, loaned by the French King, and then everything promised a successful issue for the great events in progress.

The American troops arrived in Philadelphia on the 2d of September; the French, in all the pomp and beauty and precision of military display, arrived the day after. Washington left Philadelphia September 5th, on his way to Yorktown. Having passed Chester a few miles, an express met him conveying the intelligence that De Grasse had arrived in the Chesapeake with twenty-eight ships of the line, and three thousand troops, from San Domingo.

Washington was so overjoyed that he immediately returned to Chester, to rejoice with General Rochambeau over the cheering news.

Rochambeau had reached Chester by water. They met and had a joyful dinner together.

Washington reached Elkton the next day. The troops had begun to embark, and he wrote from there to De Grasse congratulating him on his arrival, and giving him all needful information in regard to his plans and his hopes. La Fayette was to effect a junction with the troops on board the ships of De Grasse, who were under the command of the Count De St. Simon, and the French and American Armies were to coöperate to prevent the escape, and finally to defeat and capture Lord Cornwallis.

Washington and Rochambeau crossed the Susquehanna at Havre de Grace on the morning of the 8th of September, and proceeded to Baltimore. Starting early on the 9th, Washington, having Colonel Humphries with him, left Baltimore and arrived at Mt. Vernon late on the same day.

Rochambeau arrived there in the evening of the next day, and the Marquis De Chastellux and his aids, on the 11th.

Washington had not been at his own fireside since his country called him to Cambridge more than six years before.

On the 12th of September they left Mt. Vernon and, proceeding to Williamsburg, joined La Fayette.

Cornwallis, meanwhile, had been aroused to a keen sense of danger, by the appearance of De Grasse in the bay on the 28th of August, and worked diligently to strengthen his position, calling, at the same time, on Sir Henry Clinton for more troops.

De Grasse urged La Fayette to attack the British at Yorktown before their defenses were completed: but La Fayette preferred to await the arrival of General Washington, with the forces under his command, being now assured that, if De Grasse remained in the Chesapeake, the British could not be reinforced.

At this time, Admiral Graves appeared off Cape Henry, with twenty sail of British war ships, which De Grasse regarded as a challenge to come out and fight him.

De Grasse did not decline the contest, but promptly weighed anchor and put to sea with twenty-four ships.

On the 7th of September the two fleets engaged at 4 o'clock in the afternoon, when, after a severe battle, night closed the engagement.

The French had the weather gage of the adversary, and, after manœuvring in sight of each other for five days, neither party being anxious for a renewal of the fight, De Grasse, learning that a smaller French fleet had passed in the capes to the Chesapeake, returned to his anchorage in the bay, bringing with him two British frigates which he had captured.

Graves, crippled in the fight, bore away for New York. De Barras had brought with him a fleet of transports, with troops, artillery and munitions of war for the use of the Americans.

The French commander, aware of the presence of Washington and Rochambeau, and wishing to have a personal interview with them, sent the " Queen Charlotte," an elegant vessel recently captured at sea, with Lord Rawdon on board, up James River to convey the distinguished chiefs of the American Army down the bay to their vessel.

Washington, Rochambeau, Knox and Duportail proceeded to visit the French fleet on the 18th of September, and were received with the highest naval honors, the yards being manned and the national airs played by the bands of musicians on board the ships.

After agreeing upon plans to capture Cornwallis, Washington and his companions, on the same evening, again boarded the "Queen Charlotte" and started on their return to the James River; but contrary winds and storms delayed them so much that they were four days on the return passage.

At this time Admiral Digby arrived at New York with British troops and six war ships.

De Grasse, having been reinforced by the fleet of De Barras, panted for a sea fight with Digby, and proposed to take all but the ships at York River and seek him.

This would have seriously endangered the success of the campaign, for an English fleet might enter the Chesapeake at any moment, attack the four French ships at Yorktown, beat them, and bear Cornwallis and the troops away to attack us at some unprotected point. Washington was greatly disturbed at this prospect. He wrote De Grasse, urging him to remain, and made La Fayette bear the letter, in order that *his* personal appeals might give additional weight to his own arguments. De Grasse consented to remain, and it was agreed that a large part of the fleet should anchor in York River, while four or five vessels should patrol James River, to prevent Cornwallis' escape in that direction.

Clinton at this time wrote Cornwallis that twenty-three ships, under Admiral Digby, would sail from New York for his relief on the 5th of October, having, also, five thousand land troops, and directed him, on hearing heavy firing at the mouth of the bay, to send up two columns of smoke to indicate his continued occupation of Yorktown.

In his reply, Cornwallis expressed the hope that the Americans would advance, and was confident of being able to hold his position until succor arrived.

The American and French land forces numbered about twelve thousand men, exclusive of the militia of Virginia under General Nelson.

By the 9th of October the investment of the place was complete, and Washington himself applied the match to the first cannon fired on the beleaguered place.

A furious cannonade was kept up until the night of the 14th, when it was determined to storm the British works; and, for this object, a detachment was made from both the French and American Armies, the Americans commanded by La Fayette, and the French by the Baron De Viomenil.

La Fayette gave the honor of leading the advance to his trusted friend, Colonel Gimat. Colonel Hamilton loudly complained of the injustice of this, claiming the honor of leading the advance as his right, it being his tour of duty.

La Fayette's defense was the sanction Washington had given to the arrangement. Hamilton appealed by letter to Washington, who, finding it really was Hamilton's tour of duty, directed that Hamilton's wishes should be respected.

It was arranged that Colonel Gimat's battalion should lead, and that Hamilton's should follow, but that Hamilton should have command of both battalions.

Even when surrounded by suffering and death, man's nature still asserts itself, as if all was happiness and peace. Before the assault was made, the Baron De Viomenil had said to La Fayette that the French forces would accomplish their object, and would soon be in the entrenchments of the enemy, but he had some doubts as to what the untrained Americans would do.

The Americans, led by the brave Gimat and the impetuous Hamilton, captured the part of the defenses they attacked first, when La Fayette sent an aid to De Viomenil, stating that they were in the enemy's works, and asked if *he* had captured *his* part of the entrenchments, offering, also, to send the Baron help if he needed it.

De Viomenil replied, "Tell the Marquis that I am not in mine, but will be in five minutes." Cornwallis now attempted to escape, and, in the darkness of the night of October 16th, in the midst of a violent storm, he embarked a large part of his forces in boats, intending to convey all over to the Gloucester side of the river, and to fight his way to the North and join Sir Henry Clinton at New York.

Part of them had crossed, and others had embarked, but the violence of the storm drove the boats down the river and threatened their destruction. With difficulty they regained the place of embarkation, and morning found them divided by the river.

He brought back those who had crossed, and awaited the inevitable.

On the 17th he proposed to capitulate, and, after the arrangement of the terms in great detail, on the 19th the British troops marched out of Yorktown and became prisoners of war.

This expedition had a most important influence on the great contest, from which we emerged a free and happy people.

It is almost certain that if La Fayette had not been in Virginia, Cornwallis, finding himself in danger, would have retreated to the South, and it is equally probable that, but for the importunity of Washington and La Fayette, De Grasse would have left the Chesapeake in search of Admiral Graves, in which case Cornwallis, having the freedom of the waters, would have returned to Portsmouth on his transports in the way he left there.

It is highly probable that if Cornwallis had not been captured. the American Revolution would have been a failure, while it is not probable that we should have been at this day subjects of Queen Victoria; for other causes. in later times. when our strength had become more matured. would have led to independence.

In 1781 France had need of peace, and further succors could not have been expected; without them, if the campaign of 1781 had been fruitless, we should have retired disheartened from the long and bloody contest.

When the mind has been long turned back to these eventful scenes in the days that are past, and when the *great actors* in the events that were fraught with such mighty influence upon the affairs of nations are about to pass from consideration. we cannot repress a kindly interest in their later lives.

Washington. we all know, lives in the memory of the American people. and is embalmed in their heart of hearts; and we know, too, that in all the earth. wherever letters are known, and even in the abodes of the untutored savage, who knows not the true God. his name is synonomous with all that is pure and noble in human character.

All " nations, and kindred, and tongues, and people" accord him the highest niche in the temple of eternal fame.

There is a beautiful and spontaneous tribute paid to the memory of Washington that is not known, perhaps, to many of the American people.

Some years ago I was on a steamboat coming up the Potomac River. Suddenly the tolling of the steamer's bell broke the stillness of the summer night. I arose and inquired the cause of it. I was told that we were passing the tomb of Washington, and I learned that it was never omitted by steamers when in front of Mt. Vernon. There happened to be a band of musicians on board, and, when the bell ceased its tolling, they struck up the inspiring strains of "Hail, Columbia."

Until that hour I had never comprehended, in its full force, the practical fact that Washington was indeed "First in war, first in peace, and first in the hearts of his countrymen."

The second great actor in the events of 1781 was the unfortunate Louis XVI of France.

Having suffered the keenest torments that can fall to the lot of man, he filled a bloody grave with thousands of his murdered countrymen, and it is not certain that any part of his remains were found when the attempt was made in 1815 to give them honored burial beneath the temple of glory that was begun by Bonaparte.

Sir Henry Clinton had an honorable career after the American war, and died Governor of Gibraltar.

Cornwallis rose to considerable eminence, and became twice, at periods wide apart, Governor General of India, and died in India while holding that responsible place.

Rochambeau became a Marshal of France, and narrowly escaped the guillotine during the reign of terror there. Napoleon made him a grand officer of the Legion of Honor. He died in 1807.

His son, who was with him as aid in this country, became a General in the French Army, and was killed in the dreadful battle of Leipsic, in 1813.

La Fayette was one of the world's heroes. Born to aristocratic privileges, he early espoused the cause of universal equality, and drew his sword in defence of the rights of man. He possessed very considerable military talent, as his campaign in Virginia abundantly proved. He had great influence in France, which was exerted at various periods in behalf of liberty and order. He visited the United States in 1824, and was received and entertained with distinguished honor, as the guest of the nation. During his visit, Congress voted him two hundred thousand dollars, in money, and a vast tract of the public lands.

I have stated that a view of the situation of the States, and of France in 1681, justifies the belief that we could not have succeeded in that war if Cornwallis had escaped at Yorktown.

We have seen that Cornwallis' invasion of Virginia was a diversion in favor of Lord Rawdon, who was attacked in the Carolinas by General Greene.

This plan of Greene's—leaving Virginia to be succored from the North, and marching against Lord Rawdon, which induced Cornwallis to march from North Carolina to Virginia, was urged upon General Greene by General Henry Lee, the father of the soldier who led the forces of the Southern Confederacy from 1861 to 1865.

Let the descendants of these great men, not regard the liberty secured by their sacrifices as a self-acting principle.

Let us not forget that "eternal vigilance is the price of liberty," and that if that vigilance is slackened Constitutions are undermined by slow attack from the base and vicious elements that pervade all human society, until at last the fairest structures of human wisdom topple to their fall, perhaps to rise no more.

I conjure my fellow inheritors of the precious boon conferred upon us by the deeds of the great men whose actions we commemorate, to stand shoulder to shoulder in defence of every principle that belongs to our inestimable birthright.